How To Grow Your Personal Brand:
The Negotiation & Decision Way

By
Dr Gunjeet Kaur
Ph.D

Acknowledgements

I thank all the participants who have attended my seminars, coaching workshops, and corporate trainings. I also thank all who encouraged me to launch a short online course in Personal Branding that includes hands-on fully customized tools necessary to become a successful Personal Brand.

Thanks to my best friend- my daughter- for being a part of my life!

Pushed down by life many times, I thank the trust that has supported me in my bad times, ambition and achievements

Negotiation

Negotiation is a dynamic process through which two parties, each with its own objectives, agree to reach a mutually satisfying arrangement on a matter important to both the parties. We are negotiating all the time: with customers, suppliers, trade unions, family - indeed, all with whom we come into contact. In business, in particular, negotiation needs management

Negotiation is the process of reaching a solution whereas bargaining is the process where two parties agree on what they would "pay or receive". Thus, bargaining emphasizes the tangible outcome of the dialogue whereas negotiation gives a secondary importance to the tangible outcome and is more concerned with reaching an agreement which would solve the problem. The solution may be based on a combination of the tangible outcome and an intangible 'win-win' situation

The objective of an effective negotiation is not to reach a win-lose situation but a win-win situation for both the parties. An analogy can be drawn with the game of chess where "mind is pitted against mind". The difference between the game of chess and negotiation is that in the former one party wins through mental manipulations, but in the latter, both the parties have to win. They create a climate of trust that opens the door to future relationships. The important important point for individuals aiming to become and grow their Personal Brand is to focus on trust as the outcome of negotiation.

At the very beginning, it is necessary to do everything possible to reduce tensions and to express the intent for a successful outcome for all parties. Firstly, negotiating sessions are essentially composed by the harmonization and ratification of the agenda and presentation of items that will be discussed. That should create the base for negotiation process, revealing the real needs and starting positions of each party

Negotiation Process

The approach taken by various researchers is analogous to personal selling process where the salesman directly sells the company's product/service to the prospective customer. This approach is shortsighted in the sense that negotiation is taken as a process of selling one's opinions, views, and gathering information about the other party· more of bargaining than negotiation.

Rather, the negotiation process, as opposed to selling, is about reaching a closure that is based on win-win rather than one-sided sale deal. This involves stages as below:

(1) *Information Search and Analysis*

(2) *Prediction and Approximation of Result*

(3) *Your Interaction with the Other Party*

(4) Conduct of Negotiation Process

(5) Closing the 'Deal'

(6) Post-Closure Analysis

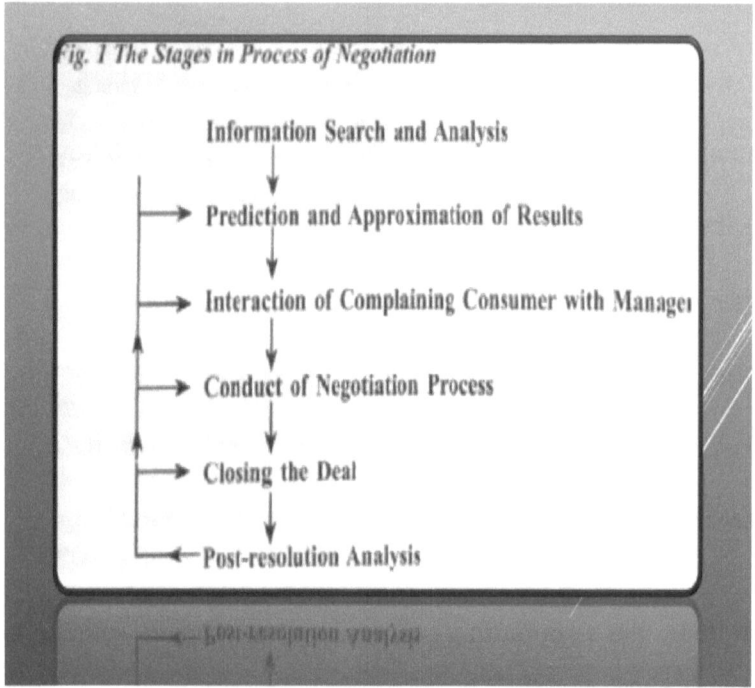

Fig. 1 The Stages in Process of Negotiation

Information Search and Analysis

→ Prediction and Approximation of Results

→ Interaction of Complaining Consumer with Manager

→ Conduct of Negotiation Process

→ Closing the Deal

←Post-resolution Analysis

(1) *Information Search and Analysis*

The first stage involves gathering   information   about

the   other   party   to negotiation. Information includes

data regarding   the   demography, response expectation

of the party and past record in your interactions, if any. The data has to be analyzed in order to find linkages in the expectations of the other party and your resources, importance of the deal to you and the other party, nature, magnitude and frequency of the implications involved in the deal, and your willingness to commit.

(2) Prediction and Approximation of Result

On the basis of an analysis of gathered data, you may make certain approximations regarding the offer, perceived as leading to other party's satisfaction. The prediction of the behavior of the other party and the probability of his acceptance of the offer would enable you to pre-decide his/her style of negotiation (controlling, collaborating, avoiding, accommodating, or compromising). Further, the approximated outcome, when compared with the actual outcome of the negotiation, would facilitate an evaluation of your perceptional abilities.

(3) Your Interaction with the Other Party

This stage is an important step towards establishing your relationship with the other party. The personal interaction will give you an impression of the behavioral styles of the person you are dealing with creating a platform for further negotiation and future interactions. The start of the negotiation is extremely important as it creates an image which is difficult to change later on. The attitude of both the parties becomes visible in this stage with observation and understanding playing a major role towards creating a successful negotiation. The perception of both verbal and non-verbal cues becomes easier and enhances the chances

(4) Conduct of Negotiation Process

You have to conduct the negotiation process in a manner which creates an impression that y o u a r e willing to reach a solution which would be beneficial to both. As your goal is to close the deal, you should focus on interactional justice leading to a smooth conduct of negotiation You must handle the objections of the other party in a manner that will satisfy the party even if he/she does not get the expected offer. During the conduct, your own implied operative rules, psychological motivators and behavioral parameters must be in balanced in order to be effective

(5) *Closing the 'Deal'*

The closure of the negotiation deserves a separate mention as a smooth or abrupt closure would make or mar the final satisfaction.. Abrupt closure might be taken as a rude dismissal or might create an impression of 'loss' in other party's mind. Giving the other party time to agree to the final package gives him/her a feeling of being a 'winner' and the 'suggestor' of the final package.

(6) Post-Closure Analysis

An analysis of the negotiation process on completion is important as it will draw your attention to your shortcomings and strengths. SWOT analysis, both yours and that of the negotiation process, can provide feedback for future negotiations and predictions for the actual outcomes of negotiation.

The Role of Your 'Decision'

A decision is a conscious choice to behave or to think in a particular manner. To take control of your own personal brand and your own success, your decisions must be based on your personal choices, strengths, and priorities. Strengths and priorities based decision making skills save you time, money and effort and generates more confidence to further your own personal brand.

We not only make decisions but also experience them- this implies that how you perceive the decisions taken by others around you impacts your own decision making skills as it becomes a factor in your future decisions. Honing perception, thus, becomes integral to decision-making and helps in influencing the decision-making of the people you want to interact with and/or close your business deal with.

To hone your perception and decision-making skills, you must understand your environment, or decision-making context. Successful approaches include

1. A deliberate categorization of people, situations or processes into any of the existing frameworks, eg complex-simple, rational-intuitive, etc

2. An understanding of and being sensitive to people's value systems,

3. Thinking of yourself as a sensing being who attempts to respond to other person's spoken and unspoken mind, and

4. Using intuition.

You adopt decision making styles, techniques, and process to reach a decision- to have and be a strong personal brand, you must develop your own personal model of decision-making based on your goals, priorities, and strengths. Constantly improving your weaknesses and blindly adopting any successful person's style may not work for you.

- **Decision making styles** refer to **personality**, thought processes, and behavioral components that are part of you, eg you can be emotional, or adopt a mixed style

- **Decision making techniques** are the specific tactics that you use to reach your decision. Eg analytical, synthesizing etc

- **Decision making process** provides a defined sequence of steps that you follow to either guide you to or take a decision eg Define, Innovate, Decide, etc

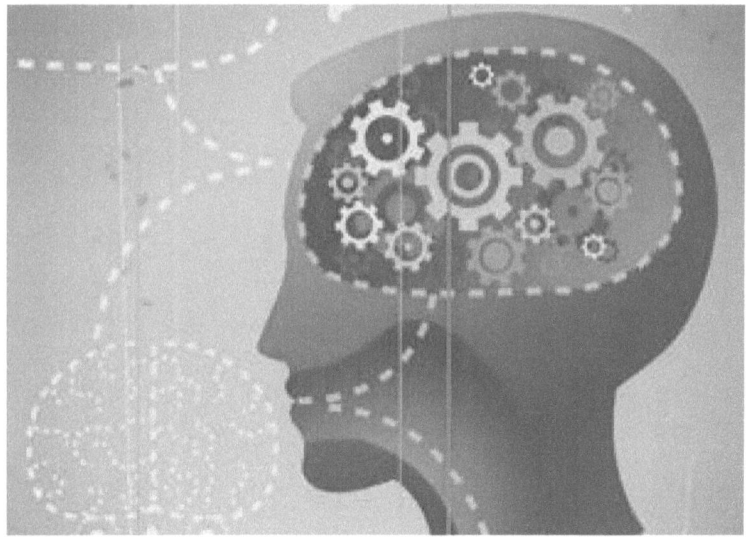

Your own personal model of decision making for creating and growing your personal brand will involve any or a mix of the decision making as listed below. You must select that mix (as depending only on one of these does not involve the whole brain that leads to a much better decision) that defines YOU. Ignorance or prejudices are two errors that you must avoid alongwith stereotypes as these program the attitude, form, style and results of a negotiation.

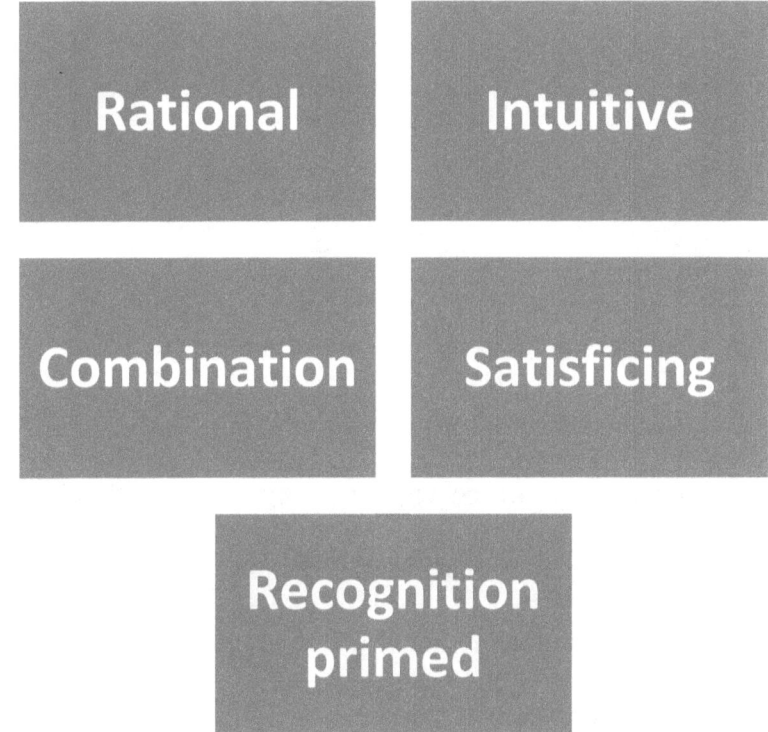

Rational

- Taught and learned, **logical and sequential** with a focus on listing alternatives and then analyzing to find the best. A major part of such decisions is the listing of pros and cons of each option in order of importance. This involves a considerable reasoning and thinking to select the optimum decision. Many of these types of decision makers create a model for themselves that has have steps in a particular sequence.

For example,

Jim's business is growing but his office is small and, in online business transactions, his portal was full. He thought of buying a bigger office and increasing the capacity of his portal to overcome that issue. He then analyzed his problem- it was not the small office or growing business but the lack of space that was the actual problem.

Jim, being a rational decision maker, thought about all alternatives:

- If I remove all extra stuff in my office that's not required, can I free up space?
- Do I have space to build a new room?
- Do I have to buy a new office?

Being an entrepreneur focused on his business, he was very particular about the most important resources he had- time and cost. He used these to evaluate his options:

Time:

- When will I need that space?
- When will solving the problem be critical?
- And how long will each option take?

Cost

- Do I have sufficient funds to buy/rent a new bigger office?
- How long will building a new room in present office solve the problem without creating impact on my profitability?
- If I have to take a loan, will my business bear the rate of

  interest?

After analyzing and evaluating his options based on these two parameters, he decided to shift to new office that had more space and also had sufficient vacant space to build another room that he may require in the future.

Intuitive

- This reverses and goes to the other extreme of logic and is based on the assumption that there is no reason or logic to the decision making process and decision is left to an inner knowing, or intuition, or some kind of sense of what the right thing to do is. This is described as "I can feel it in their heart" or "in my bones", or " in my gut" etc.

For example,

Cathy faced falling demand for her products in her small online business and high employee turnover, so she did something that her friends called a foolish decision- she doubled her employees' salaries. Within a year, turnover dropped by 60% while productivity nearly doubled. This increased the sales as it made her employees more happy. When asked, she said "I just had a hunch this will work so I went ahead and implemented it".

Combination

- A mix of rational and intuitive processes- may ne deliberately adopted or learnt. Eg, you list the pros and cons of the options, assign priority to each, and analyze to reach a decision (The rational part.) But you are not satisfied, feel uneasy somehow (the intuitive part), so you change the priorities, and the analysis throws up a different decision that is somehow more 'satisfactory'.

For example,

Mike wanted a promotion in her present job but could not think of a way to talk to her boss. She analyzed her problem, found that he was scared to talk to his boss because she had a tough personality. He found that the problem was his own fear of getting insulted or thrown out of job. He analyzed and evaluated his options in a rational manner by listing the pros and cons of talking to her- he found that the worst case scenario was being thrown out of his job. He also was aware that till date the attrition rate in his company was very low.

He decided to wait for a day before talking to her and got busy in his work. In the evening he met his boss in the elevator and started talking to her about promotion. She smiled and promised that she will think about it. Next day she called him and gave him the promotion letter with increment and better incentives.

Mike could not explain why he talked with her in the elevator- he said "Something just told me to talk to her so I talked". So he used a combination style of decision making

Satisficing

This is where people pick the first decision that will give the result. Often a 'good enough' option given your top satisfaction parameters and sacrifices other potentially better options.

For example,

Sharon had just launched her business and was searching for a wholesale buyer to distribute her line of designer apparels. She talked to 6 of them and decided on one of them quickly as that buyer fulfilled most of her important criteria.

Recognition primed decision making

Gather information from environment vis-à-vis the decision we want to make, select an option that we think will work, rehearse it mentally and if we think it works, we go ahead. If it doesn't work, we choose another decision, repeat this process, and continue this entire process till we get to the right decision.

For example,

Sandra received two employment offers simultaneously. She could not decide which one to select so she imagined herself in the first organization after gathering information about the company through her sources. She found that she could not imagine herself in that company as the company was located in the outskirts of a city and was surrounded by rural area. She tried the second option and found that it was much better than the first and near-fitted her requirement. She refused the first offer even though they were providing perks like free meals, free conveyance, and a bigger office room.

Importance of Time

An agreement to negotiate is a necessary but not a sufficient condition for solution. A variable, which assumes an important dimension, is the time frame within which the decision has to be taken. Time at our disposal is limited and a choice has to made from among the uses to which it can be put. The importance of time is further highlighted in the concept of 'bounded rationality' which propounds that decisions have to be taken within the limitations imposed by human cognitions and time

Time can be divided into two categories:

(I) Time Resource Constraint, which refers to the total time available, and

(2) Time Consumption Constraint, which refers to the time available for a particular activity.

In the context of negotiation, you should set the time limits within which the outcome has to be achieved. Since the decision is a 'cut' signifying the irrevocability of that moment of time, the decision has to be taken carefully as going back would be at the cost of personal and your business's credibility.

The 'timing' constituent involves being perceptive in recognizing the right time to start the process, make an offer, and reach a solution. people tend to make more conservative decisions when outcomes occurred soon after the decision than when outcome occurred farther into the future (i.e. a week or more). It all depends upon the need for decision, its urgency, importance, and cost.

"Cues": The Core of Negotiation

Cue is a signal to start speaking, acting or doing something; an indication of the 'right time'. In negotiation, cues are that moment of time where an action taken, or a word spoken, reaps in rewards which exceed the cost of negotiation. Identification of the cues at each stage of negotiation is important but their significance becomes particularly more relevant' at the interaction, conduct and closure stages of negotiation.

The cues highlight the importance of time and their correct identification leads to a successful negotiation. The correct identification of cues involves a knowledge of motivation, perception, and learning aspects of consumer behavior. Cues are reflected through two clues:

(I) verbal clues- are evident from style of talking, content matter of the discussion, and time taken to reach the 'heart' of the matter

(2) non-verbal clues. include posture, expression, mode of dress, and body language.

An underlying important factor, enabling a correct recognition of cues, is perception which involves observation and listening. Perception is the process of attributing meaning, on the basis of past experience, to the stimuli received through five senses. The assimilation of the stimuli and its interpretation is, therefore, subjective

Response expectation of the other party you are dealing with usually centers on three types of rewards for engaging in negotiation with you:

1. Distributive Justice- the tangibles expected
2. Procedural Justice- time taken to understand him/her and close the deal or make an offer
3. Interactional Justice- empathy, fairness, courtesy, understanding you show while communicating.

Deals in entrepreneurial and personal branding world have highlighted the importance of procedural and interactional

Justices for successful handling of the other party and closure of the deal. An understanding of these two important constituents of the expectation mix is a starting point in the negotiation process and should form an integral part of information search and analysis stage of the process. The meeting with is the stage which involves maximum attention to your perceptual abilities to make an offer that consists of a solution reached after combining the expectations of the other party and the objective conclusions drawn on the basis of perceived cues.

Cues play an important role while matching the expectations with the offer. Sound perception based on observation and learning through the cues will enable you to adapt and synchronize with the other party. Your perception will usually categorize other party's behavior in two categories:

1. "Goalistic" behavior, that results when the other party directly addresses the most important criteria and priorities of engaging with you (in case of job, contracts etc) or of buying your product/service. The purpose is to achieve effectiveness in the process and obtain the end result, and

2. "Individualist" behavior, that results when the other party does not directly address the priorities but indulges in negotiation to enhance self-esteem

Collaborating style, known as the best style of becoming a Personal Brand, enhances your creativity and leads to a 'win• win' situation- you can inculcate this style by attempting to achieve your as well as the other party's goals and still maintain inter-personal relations.

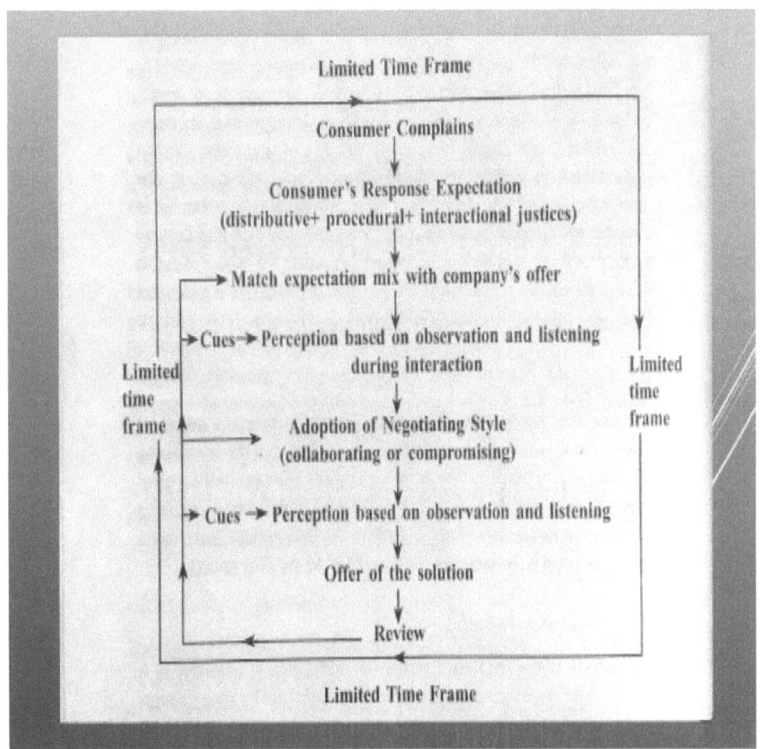

For example,

John had an export business and was negotiating with his buyer in the US. The buyer quoted a price of $6.34 per piece for every piece of cosmetic jewelery that John was exporting. John had sent him a quotation for $8.50 as this price covered his costs and gave him a margin of $1.25 per piece after keeping in mind the negotiation that he knew will take place. He had expected that the buyer will quote around $7.45 as this was a trend in his industry. He found the quoted price too low.

However, the buyer had an excellent reputation in the industry and had a track record of quick sales and easy payments coming back. He decided to engage in collaborative style of negotiation- he and the buyer discussed the prices, analyzed each other's reasons for quoting their prices. They finally mutually decided to close the deal in a manner that gave both of them safety margins to cover the risks- at $7. This created a win-win situation for both though gave John a lower profitability but resulted in a long term relationship with the buyer.

The compromising style assumes that a win-win situation is not possible and you then adopts a stance where y o u r goals are adjusted to suit the other party . This solution is 'satisficing' within the assumptions of bounded rationality- usually adopted by fresh small non-funded start up entrepreneurs, individuals in need of offer, or those giving extreme importance to time.

It is possible and acceptable for y o u to adopt any styles of negotiation, based on the inherent characteristic of 'win-win' stance of collaborating approach and 'mini-win-mini-lose' stance of compromising approach (operative word being "mini"). The above-mentioned characteristics of the approaches enable you to sharpen y o u r ability to not only achieve your goals but also the o t h e r p a r t y ' s goals. This becomes particularly relevant in the relationship context where one deal can lead to continuous business.

Keeping in mind the importance of these critical factors, you must

1. Be Ready to walk away and "play poker"- You must develop an ability to play poker with the other party, and be able to walk away if you do not like the terms of the deal. Small start up entrepreneurs without funding, people with financial responsibilities are an exception to this tactic. Know before you start what your offer/expectation isand pre-decide the lowest offer that you will accept.

2. Avoid "negotiating by continually conceding." Giving in continuously to demands of the other party just so that you can close the deal will encourage the other party to make unreasonable demands, run you into losses, create your personal brand as an " easy sucker" , and a desperate fool.

3. Know that time is the enemy of many deals. You have to keep in mind hat the longer a deal takes to get completed, the more likely that you will either give in to unreasonable demands or the other party will lose interest. So be prompt in responding, and keep the deal momentum going. However, rushing through negotiations and make concessions also makes time your enemy.

Implications for Your Personal Brand

YOUR BRAND IS WHAT OTHER PEOPLE SAY ABOUT YOU WHEN YOU'RE NOT IN THE ROOM.

Jeff Bezos, CEO of Amazon

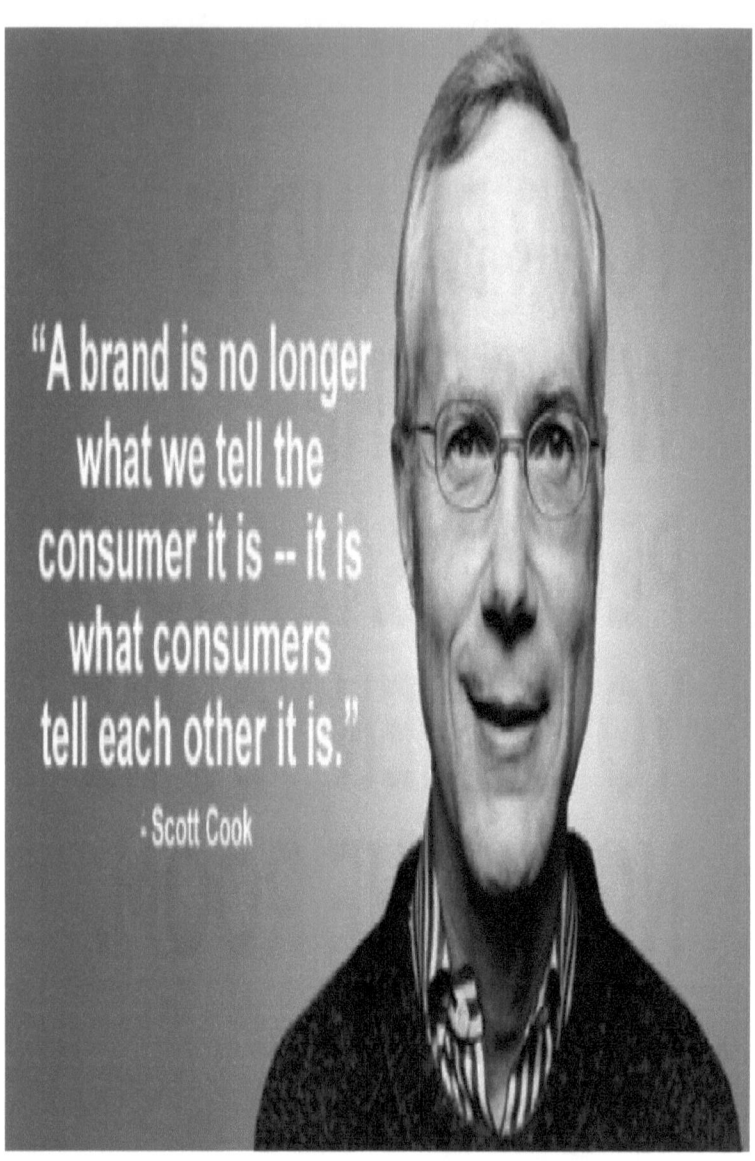

The interactional justice based suggestions and process based on time and cues are extremely strong way to ensure the growth of your personal brand. Emphasis on interactional justice and a sharp focus on the time frame will make negotiation process more efficient and effective. This guarantees that the satisfied other party indulges in positive word-of-mouth, repurchase of your product/service and becomes brand loyal. The brand loyalty becomes the basis of a relationship and enhances your image in the target market.

An understanding of the suggested process will make you a perceptive negotiator with confidence to improve your brand and create a 'Humane' image of being someone who looks at and treats the other humans less as a 'money- machine' and more as a human beings who deserve to be treated as an 'individual'

Moreover, the suggested process of negotiation, with its linkages drawn between three types of justice and time frame and cues, will help you to develop your interactive skills and the ability to communicate effectively. A thorough understanding of the process will also enable an identification of the right justice mix expected by the other party and an easy identification of cues. This develops your ability to recognize the other party's specific feelings, values, and beliefs about proper conduct in negotiation, and to synchronize your attitude and behavior to the issues and personalities involved in the particular d e a l .

You will be enabled to customize your communication and put across your requirements in a manner to negotiate more efficiently with your goals as your priority. This will enable you to be focused on your target customer/boss/colleague, your personal brand definition, and goals.

Communicate for Your Growth, Not for Just Getting

Dr Gunjeet Kaur

www.ingramcontent.com/pod-product-compliance
Lightning Source LLC
Chambersburg PA
CBHW030738180526
45157CB00008BA/3217